STAR FILES

Mike Myers

Paul Harrison

Raintree

Chicago, Illinois

© 2005 Raintree, a division of Reed Elsevier Inc.
Chicago, Illinois

Customer Service 888-363-4266

Visit our website at www.raintreelibrary.com

For more information address the publisher:
Raintree, 100 N. LaSalle, Suite 1200, Chicago IL 60602

Printed and bound in China by South China Printing Company

09 08 07 06 05
10 9 8 7 6 5 4 3 2 1

Library of Congress Cataloging-in-Publication Data

Harrison, Paul, 1969-
  Mike Myers / Paul Harrison.
      p. cm. -- (Star files)
  Includes bibliographical references and index.
  ISBN 1-4109-1088-1 (lib. bndg.)
  1. Myers, Mike, 1963---Juvenile literature. 2. Motion picture actors and actresses--Canada--Biography--Juvenile literature. I. Title. II. Series.
  PN2308.M94H37 2005
  792.702'8'092--dc22

                    2004011261

Acknowledgements
The publishers would like to thank the following for permission to reproduce photographs: Allstar Picture Library pp. **4**, **19** (l), **19** (r), **20**, **21** (l), **21** (r), **22**, **23** (l), **25**, **27** (l), **27** (r), **28**, **29** (l), **35** (r), **37** (r), **38** (r), **40**, **41** (l); Corbis pp. **8** (r), **13** (l), **13** (r), **36**, **43** (l); Getty Images pp. **6** (l), **9**, **32**, **34** (r), **42**; Retna Pictures pp. **12**, **15** (l), **33** (r); Rex Features pp. **6** (r), **7**, **8** (l), **10**, **11** (l), **11** (r), **14**, **15** (r), **16** (l), **16** (r), **17** (l), **17** (r), **18** (l), **23** (r), **24**, **26**, **29** (r), **30**, **31** (l), **31** (r), **33** (l), **34** (l), **35** (l), **37** (l), **38** (l), **39**, **41** (r), **43** (r). Cover photograph reproduced with permission of Starmax Inc.

Quote sources: pp. **4**, **10**, **14**, **36**, **42** Entertainers with Byron Allen, Entertainmentstudios.com; pp. **12**, **18**, **19**, **24** *Wayne's World* DVD; pp. **12** *Mike Myers* by Lonnie Hull DuPont; p. **22**, **23**, **24** *Austin Powers in Goldmember* DVD; p. **24** *Austin Powers: The Spy Who Shagged Me* DVD; p. **25** Liese Spencer *Sight and Sound*; p. **25** Tom Long *The Detroit News*; p. **26** Interview at *Austin Powers in Goldmember* premiere; p. **41** Internet Movie Database.

The publishers would like to thank Voirrey Carr and Simone Apel for their assistance in the preparation of this book.

Disclaimer: This book is not authorized or approved by Mike Myers.

Contents

Suburbs Superstar   4

Starting Out   8

Highs and Lows   18

Yeah Baby, Yeah   26

Behind the Scenes   32

A Monster Hit   38

The Cat in the Hat   40

Future Plans   42

Find Out More   *44*

Glossary   *46*

Index   *48*

Some words are shown in bold, **like this**. You can find out what they mean by looking in the glossary. You can also look out for them in the "Star Words" box at the bottom of each page.

Suburbs Superstar

Mike Myers was a short, shy, geeky child from a quiet city in Canada who dreamed of being a comedian. He is now one of the most popular actors, writers, and comedians of his day.

One of Mike's most famous characters is Austin Powers.

Old and new

In many ways, Mike is like an old-fashioned **variety show** star. He can sing, he can dance, he can act, and he is very funny. Mike combines all these elements and makes them feel fresh and modern. Mike is a very physical performer. He loves **slapstick** humor. Slapstick is one of the most basic forms of humor.

ALL ABOUT MIKE

Full name: Michael Myers
Born: May 25, 1963
Place of birth: Scarborough, Ontario
Family: Father Eric; mother Alice; brothers Peter and Paul
Height: 5' 7" (1.7 meters)
Hobbies: Ice hockey and music
Married: Robin Ruzan (1993)
Big break: Joining the television program *Saturday Night Live* in 1988
First major movie: *Wayne's World*
Other interests: Has pet dogs and plays in a band

Star Words

4

variety show mixture of songs, dances, and comedy
slapstick people falling over or being hit in a funny way

Here is Mike in a typical pose.

What is Mike's favorite sport?

Mike is also a master of making up comedy as he goes along. This is called **improvising**.

Which character did Mike play in his first major movie?

Hard-working genius

Mike is difficult to classify. What is clear is that he is a comedy star. So how did Mike go from **suburbs** to superstar? The answer is simple. It took a bit of luck, a lot of hard work, and a large slice of genius.

> What I'd like to do is something extraordinary.

What movies inspired *Austin Powers*?

improvise make things up as you go along
suburbs outskirts of a town or city where people live

Toronto lies by the side of Lake Ontario.

Home town boy

Mike grew up in Scarborough, Canada. This is a **suburb** of Toronto, which is a very large city. Scarborough was not a glamorous place. It just had the usual shopping malls and fast-food restaurants. Later, Mike used this ordinary place as the **inspiration** for some of his work.

Leaving Liverpool

Mike's parents moved to Canada from Liverpool, England, in 1956. At that time people were being encouraged to **emigrate** from the United Kingdom to Canada to start new lives there.

Simple childhood

Much of Mike's childhood was spent playing with his brothers in the basement of his house. As he got older, Mike became a typical suburban teenager. He took trips into town with his friends. They ate burgers and donuts, and listened to music.

Mike was awarded a star on the Hollywood Walk of Fame in 2002. His mother, Alice, and wife, Robin, went with him to the ceremony.

Star Words   inspiration where you get your ideas from

The Beatles were the world's favorite band when Mike was a child.

Number three

Mike's family was very close. Mike was the youngest of three boys. He was often picked on by his older brothers, Peter and Paul. Mike's parents even believed that Peter and Paul were funnier than Mike. Nevertheless, Mike's mother spotted his ability to entertain people. She did not want Mike just to be the family clown, however. She encouraged him to take dancing lessons from an early age.

 Star fact

Mike got lots of helpful hints and tips from his mother, Alice. She had trained as an actress, and she could also dance.

Beatlemania

The Beatles were from Liverpool, like Mike's parents. They were also the only people Mike knew of who sounded like his mum and dad. So, Mike thought he must be related to The Beatles!

emigrate to leave one country and move to another

Starting Out

Drew Barrymore was one of the stars of the film *E.T. The Extra-Terrestrial*.

Mike's dancing lessons led to him being invited to **audition** for television commercials. When he was eight he danced in a commercial for a car company. Mike also made commercials for soft drinks and candy companies. He made guest appearances on television programs, too.

Friends on set

When Mike was nine, he appeared in a commercial for an electricity company. An actress called Gilda Radner played Mike's mother in the commercial. Mike and Gilda got on really well on **set**. Mike's brothers used to tease him about this.

Gilda Radner (center, wearing sunglasses) with other members of the *Saturday Night Live* cast.

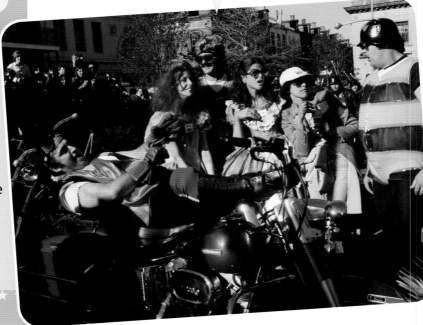

Child stars

Many top film stars worked on television programs or films when they were children. The list includes Jodie Foster, Christina Ricci, and Drew Barrymore.

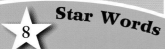

Star Words

audition interview for an actor or musician, where they show their skills

They said that Gilda was his "girlfriend." At that time neither Mike nor Gilda was famous, but Gilda later became a major comedy star.

Saturday Night Live

One night Mike was watching television with his family. A show came on called *Saturday Night Live*. It was a new type of comedy program. It had lots of funny skits and characters. It went on to become one of the most successful American comedy series ever. Mike recognized one of the stars of *Saturday Night Live*—it was Gilda Radner. Mike told his family that he would be on the program one day, too. They thought Mike was being silly. How wrong they were.

Not so special

In 1977, when Mike was fourteen, he appeared in his first movie. This was a short children's film called *Range Rider and the Calgary Kid*. The movie was like an old-fashioned western. Unfortunately, it was not a success. This experience did not discourage Mike, though. He was not going to give up. Bigger breaks were just around the corner.

Comedy and tragedy

Gilda Radner was a popular comic actress. She made her name with the comedy **troupe**, Second City. Then she starred on *Saturday Night Live* and had her own one-woman show. She won an **Emmy Award** in 1978. Sadly, Gilda died of cancer in 1989. She was just 42.

Gilda Radner was awarded a Hollywood Walk of Fame star in 2003. That was fourteen years after she died.

Mike worked hard at school. English and history were two of his favorite subjects. He was well known for missing early classes because he was still in bed. Mike was not lazy, though. Around this time, Mike went to workshops at Second City. This was a famous comedy **troupe**. Second City was based in Chicago, Illinois, but also had a troupe in Toronto.

Dan Aykroyd was a star at both Second City and *Saturday Night Live*.

A dilemma

Mike was about to leave school in 1982, so he applied to college. He was accepted. On the day of his last high school exam he **auditioned** for a place with Second City. He was accepted there, too. Mike wondered what to do. Should he continue his education or try to become a comedian? His dream of being a comedian won. He decided to join Second City.

Stars of Second City

Many famous comedians worked at Second City, both in Chicago and Toronto. These include John Candy, Dan Aykroyd, Bill Murray, and Eugene Levy.

Second City

At Second City the comedians did not learn lines or rehearse routines. Instead, they **improvised** sketches on the spot. Mike proved to be an excellent improviser. He soon became one of Second City's star performers.

"Being adaptive is the most crucial lesson I've learned."

Star Words   adapt make changes because of differing circumstances

British comedian Neil Mullarkey was an early comic partner for Mike.

Adapt or die!

Mike was very good at improvised comedy. For this, you need have to have a quick brain. There are no scripts. You never know what each person will say next. You have to be able to **adapt**. If you cannot adapt, you will not be funny.

Mike has always been an energetic performer.

Bound for Britain

Mike was at Second City for a few years. Then he wanted to try something new. In 1985 he decided to try his luck in the United Kingdom, where his parents came from. Mike performed in small comedy clubs there. He also teamed up with a British comedian called Neil Mullarkey. Together they got a regular slot on a children's television program called *The Wide Awake Club*. They even had their own series, called *Mullarkey and Myers*.

11

Wayne's World

Wayne Campbell is Mike's oldest comic character. "I used to do the character at parties when I was about 11 or 12, through my **formative years**," says Mike. Wayne is like a typical North American teenager, who loves rock music. The only difference is that Wayne made his own television program in his parents' basement.

Television in Toronto

Mike spent some time in England, but then he started to get homesick. He returned to Toronto in 1986, and joined up with the Second City team again. While performing there, he was spotted by some television **producers**. Mike was given the chance to be a television star on a new comedy show. The program was called *It's Only Rock and Roll*. Each episode was a mix of music and comedy, and lasted for half an hour.

> " Wayne is sort of like everyone I grew up with. "

Here is an early picture of Mike as Wayne Campbell.

Star Words

formative years years that shape your character

Chicago is known as the Windy City.

Mike was one of the star performers. Audiences loved two of his characters in particular. These were a German television presenter, called Dieter, and a teenage heavy metal fan, called Wayne Campbell. These characters would be important in Mike's later career.

The Windy City

It's Only Rock and Roll finished in 1987, when Mike was 24. Mike was then invited to work with the Second City **troupe** in Chicago. Chicago is also known as the Windy City. Coming from Canada, Mike was used to the icy winter weather. He loved being in Chicago.

A breath of fresh air

Second City Chicago was a very **prestigious** comedy troupe. It had a long and proud history. In recent years it had been in a slump. The show had become a bit stale. Mike helped to liven it up again. Mike did not stay with Second City for very long, though.

Waiting for inspiration

The character of Dieter was based on a German waiter Mike knew in Toronto. Dieter was weird, a bit scary, and shouted at odd times. Mike has no idea whether the waiter ever saw Mike's Dieter character.

Mike as Dieter, looking typically serious.

prestigious having a good reputation

Award winner

Mike's comedy partner, Dana Carvey, is famous in the United States for his work on *Saturday Night Live*. Dana first appeared on the show in 1986, and won an **Emmy** in 1993 for his performances.

Dana Carvey was a star on *Saturday Night Live* even before Mike arrived.

In late 1988 Mike took a week off from Second City in Chicago. He went back to Canada to celebrate the fifteenth anniversary of Second City in Toronto. Mike did a comedy performance at the party. The guests found it very funny. A man named Lorne Michaels heard about Mike. Lorne was in charge of the famous American television comedy program *Saturday Night Live*. Lorne decided to see Mike for himself.

A dream come true

Lorne met Mike and was very impressed. He offered Mike a job with *Saturday Night Live* as a writer and performer. This was a dream come true. Mike had told his family that he would be on the program years earlier. Now he was on his way to New York to be a star.

Shy boy

Working on *Saturday Night Live* was a **daunting** experience for Mike. He knew all of the cast members, because he had seen them on television. Mike was an unknown, so he was a little shy and nervous for the first few weeks.

> " I always wanted to be on Saturday Night Live. "

Here's Wayne

Things changed four weeks after Mike started. He introduced one of his favorite old characters, Wayne Campbell. Audiences loved Wayne.

Star Words

daunting when a task seems hard or scary

Star fact

Mike worked on *Saturday Night Live* for six years between 1989 and 1995. He received an Emmy Award in 1989 for his writing on the program.

Mike proved to the *Saturday Night Live* **veterans** that he had what it took. Mike got a regular slot for Wayne each week.

Dynamic duo

Wayne had a sidekick called Garth Algar. Garth was played by the comedian Dana Carvey. Mike and Dana worked very well together on screen. They would go on to have more success with their two teenage characters.

Dana Carvey, Lorne Michaels, and Mike.

Saturday stars

Lots of famous comedians have worked on *Saturday Night Live*, including Chevy Chase, James Belushi, Eddie Murphy, Adam Sandler, and Will Ferrell.

veteran person with a lot of experience in something

Modest star

Despite the many fans that Mike has won, he does not take his success for granted. He says: "I still believe that at any time the no-talent police will come and arrest me."

Movie star Bruce Willis was one of Mike's famous guests.

Mike has millions of fans around the world. He also has a large number of celebrity fans. When Mike was on *Saturday Night Live*, he got celebrities to appear with him. Lots of people wanted to be one of Mike's guests on the program. These included Aerosmith, Mick Jagger, Danny DeVito, Wayne Gretzky, Bruce Willis, Tom Hanks, and John Goodman.

Rock legends Aerosmith were among the famous stars who appeared with Mike on *Saturday Night Live*.

Surprise guest

Usually Mike knew who would be appearing on the show, but one night he got a surprise. He was playing one of his most popular characters, Linda Richman.

Mike knew he already had Madonna and Roseanne Barr on the show. They were great guests, so he was not expecting anyone else.

Struck dumb

During the sketch Linda was talking about her favorite star, the famous singer Barbra Streisand. Then, in the middle of the sketch, who should walk past in the background? Streisand herself. Mike was stunned and speechless. The motor-mouth quick-witted comedian was lost for words. It made great television.

Madonna in disguise on *Saturday Night Live*.

On tour

Singing star Barbra Streisand (above) loved the character of Linda Richman. She thought Linda was so funny that she invited Mike to join her on tour. She wanted him to play Linda as a warm-up for the crowd. Mike was thrilled to accept.

Highs and Lows

Wayne's World **costar** Rob Lowe is a close friend of Mike's.

Wayne's World

Wayne was a great success on *Saturday Night Live*. Then Mike wanted to try to make a movie of his favorite character. This would be Mike's first major movie. It was a big gamble. Turning a short television skit into a movie is very difficult. Mike would not just be acting in the movie either. He would be cowriting it as well. This was a lot of work.

The plot

Wayne and Garth have their own television series, called *Wayne's World*. It is very popular with teenagers. An evil executive, played by Rob Lowe, tries to take over *Wayne's World*. He nearly succeeds, but the boys win out in the end.

Deadline

Mike was faced with another problem, too. The filming had to be completed during the summer break of *Saturday Night Live*. This meant the movie had to be made in just 34 days. This is a very short amount of time to make a movie. If Mike felt nervous about his task, he did not show it. He was used to writing and **broadcasting** episodes of *Saturday Night Live* in a week. So, 34 days sounded like a long time.

Worried man

Mike did not feel so calm when shooting was finished. He saw an early print of the film and was convinced it would be a flop. He said: "I couldn't stand it. I couldn't watch it. I thought it was awful. I was **inconsolable**." Luckily, Mike was wrong about the movie.

Smash hit

Wayne's World was the surprise hit of 1992. Audiences loved the silliness of the movie and loved the characters of Wayne and Garth. The movie was even popular in countries that had never seen *Saturday Night Live*.

> "Wayne and Garth make everything fun. (Dana Carvey)"

Wayne loves hockey, just like Mike.

Waynespeak
Wayne's favourite sayings:
"party on"
"excellent!"
"we're not worthy"
"schwing!"

Wayne and Garth in action.

inconsolable unable to be cheered up

★ ★ ★ ★ ★ ★ ★ ★ ★ ★

Dual parts

Mike had two parts in *So I Married an Axe Murderer*. He played the main lead, Charlie Mackenzie, and his father. Mike based the father on his own dad, Eric.

★ ★ ★ ★ ★ ★ ★ ★ ★ ★

Mike as Charlie Mackenzie in *So I Married an Axe Murderer*.

Mike's next movie, called *So I Married an Axe Murderer*, did not enjoy the same success as *Wayne's World*. Mike played the lead character in this comedy movie. The script had been written and rewritten a few times before Mike read it. He thought that it could be funnier, so decided to rewrite it himself. Sometimes he was still writing a scene on the day that it was being filmed.

A flop

So I Married an Axe Murderer has lots of fans. Not enough people went to see it at the cinema for it to be a **commercial success**, though. Compared to the success of *Wayne's World*, it looked like a flop. It was a different kind of movie and story from *Wayne's World*.

Pressure

In Hollywood, if one movie is a success, there is a lot of pressure to make a **sequel**. *Wayne's World* was a big hit and people expected there to be a sequel. Sequels are sometimes not as good as the original movies, however. This turned out to be the case with *Wayne's World 2*.

★ Star fact

Mike rewrote the script for *So I Married an Axe Murderer* with his old comedy partner, Neil Mullarkey.

Star Words

commercial success something that sells well and makes a good profit

Mike and his *Axe Murderer* **co-star**, Nancy Travis.

Good points

Wayne's World 2 was not a big success, but it still has many fans. Like *Wayne's World* the movie pokes fun at television programs and other films. Then there are the special **catchphrases** and guest appearances.

Success . . . not!

Wayne's World 2 was not as successful as the first movie. The ideas were fun and fresh the first time around, but seemed stale the second time. Also, the whole idea for the movie had to be changed just weeks before filming began because of legal reasons.

A hilarious scene from *Wayne's World 2*.

Take a break

It was hard for Mike when his movies were not successful. Mike's friends advised him to take a proper break. Mike left *Saturday Night Live* and did not take on any new movies for a while.

sequel follow up
catchphrase saying linked with a certain character

Laughs from the past

Mike still loves the old comedy programs that his dad introduced him to. "I am a huge Peter Sellers fan," he says. Sellers was in many movies, including the popular *Pink Panther* series.

★ ★ ★ ★ ★ ★ ★ ★ ★

Peter Sellers as his most famous character, Inspector Clouseau.

Mike and his dad

Mike experienced personal sadness at this time, too. Mike's father Eric died just before *Wayne's World* became a huge success. He never saw Mike's great triumph.

Mike came from a very close family. He loved and trusted his parents. "I used to tell him everything," said Mike of his father. The fact he was no longer there to share things with was very painful for Mike.

Happy household

Eric had a big influence on Mike. He taught Mike and his brothers that humor was a great cure for the troubles of life. Eric loved to laugh. He was always making jokes. It was no surprise that one of his sons grew up to be a comedian.

Late-night listening

Eric Myers introduced Mike and his brothers to the best of British comedy. The Myers family loved to listen to classic radio comedy shows, or watch the television program *Monty Python's Flying Circus*. These programs were zany, lively, and **chaotic**.

★ Star fact

Mike's dad taught him **cockney** rhyming slang. This is a way of talking where a word is replaced by another word or words that rhyme with it. So, instead of saying "stairs" you say "apples and pears." Instead of saying "telephone" you say "dog and bone."

★ **Star Words**

cockney people from East London in England are called cockneys

The shows **inspired** many later comedians. They were also some of Eric's favorite programs. They provided a great comic education for Mike, too.

Some of the Monty Python cast in the movie *Monty Python and the Holy Grail*.

Back to England

Eric wanted his ashes to be taken back to Liverpool, England, when he died. Eric always thought of Liverpool as his real home. Mike's family scattered Eric's ashes on the River Mersey (above). Mike said he thought that this was the best thing he had ever done.

★ ★ ★ ★ ★ ★ ★ ★ ★ ★

chaotic confused and lacking order

Mike has always worked very hard. He is also famous for **improvising** during filming. Mike calls this making it "funnier than written." However, he still wants his scripts to be as funny as possible.

Late nights

Mike often worked late into the night when he was writing his material. This was especially true when he was working on *Saturday Night Live*. The writers would meet on a Tuesday to discuss ideas. They then had to get material ready by Friday for **rehearsal**. There was very little time to put each program together. Even the quickest writers were pushed for time. Sometimes Mike ended up sleeping in the building.

Mike often worries about his work.

Worried writer

Often Mike will do draft after draft of his work. He is never sure if it is good enough. "I sit and I worry and I rewrite madly," says Mike.

 Star fact

When Mike first worked on *Saturday Night Live* as a writer, he did not have an office, or even a desk to work at. It is said that he sat on the floor by the elevators to write his material. Mike worked his way up to having a desk. Eventually, he got his own office.

Rocket fuel

Mike is very serious about his work. Dana Carvey thinks that Mike's drive was really important when making *Wayne's World*. "Mike's obsession for detail and work ethic really was the rocket **propellant** for the movie," he says.

> The only thing I hate about movies is getting up early.

Mike as club owner Steve Rubell in *54*.

Acting up

When Mike does something, he likes to do it well. It was no surprise then that when he tried serious acting, he was very good at it. His first attempt was in 1998 in a movie called *54*. It was hard to believe that it really was Mike playing the character of Steve Rubell. He was the owner of the nightclub Studio 54. Audiences were not used to seeing Mike play straight roles. Also, he had a wig and a false nose, and looked very different.

New character

Before taking on the part in *54*, Mike had taken his friends' advice to have a break. For a while Mike did no writing or performing. It is very difficult for a hard worker like Mike to stop thinking about work, though. He was soon trying to decide what he would do next. By 1997 he was back with a new character. Mike was about to hit the big time again.

Winning performance

The movie *54* was not a success, but Mike got good reviews. One critic said, "Mike Myers' Rubell is the best thing about the movie." Another said: "Myers is wonderful as nightclub owner Steve Rubell."

Yeah Baby, Yeah

Famous friends

In the first Austin Powers movie Mike plays both Austin and Dr. Evil. Mike also wrote the script and was one of the **producers**. Another of the movie's producers was Hollywood star Demi Moore.

In 1997 Mike was back with a new character and a new movie, *Austin Powers: International Man of Mystery*. Mike did not know if people would like it. After all, his last two movies had been disappointing. He should not have worried. The movie was the comedy hit of the year.

Old inspiration

Austin Powers was **inspired** by some of Mike's favorite films from the 1960s. The biggest influences were the James Bond movies and other spy movies. In the movie Mike plays 1960s British secret agent Austin Powers. Austin was frozen in the 1960s, so he can return in the 1990s. He does battle with his rival, the **villain** Dr. Evil. Both Austin and Dr. Evil have problems adjusting to life in the 1990s. This leads to some very amusing situations. The movie was fun for Mike to make, as well. He said that Dr. Evil was his favorite character in the film because he "always wanted to play a bad guy."

Back on top

Austin Powers: International Man of Mystery really caught the public's imagination. They loved the characters and the new **catchphrases**, such as "Yeah, baby!" and "Oh, behave." Mike was a star again.

Demi Moore helped Mike to bring *Austin Powers* to the screen.

Star Words

villain character who is bad

Star fact

During a **screening** of *Austin Powers*, the film actually broke. Mike rushed to the front of the theater. He entertained the audience until the film could be repaired. The audience loved it!

Dr. Evil is one of Mike's greatest characters.

Copy cat

Mike copied some of the most famous Bond villains. Dr. Evil is based on the cat-loving Ernst Blofeld, who appears in several of the Bond movies. Both of these characters are bald and speak with an odd accent. The character Random Task is a send-up of Bond villain Odd Job from *Goldfinger*.

Mike with **costar** Elizabeth Hurley.

Legal problems

Not everyone is a fan of the Austin Powers movies. The people who make the James Bond movies wanted Mike to change the name of *Austin Powers in Goldmember*. They thought the name was too close to the Bond movie, *Goldfinger*. Mike was eventually allowed to use the title, though.

The success continues

The first Austin Powers movie was a great success. This meant that people expected **sequels**. Despite the bad experience of *Wayne's World 2*, Mike wanted to try it. In fact, Mike made two more Austin Powers movies.

Lost mojo

The first sequel was called *Austin Powers: The Spy Who Shagged Me*. In this movie Austin has his life force, or mojo, stolen. Powers has to travel back in time to stop the theft from happening. He is helped by Felicity, played by Heather Graham. The movie features the first appearance of Mini Me, the tiny Dr. Evil lookalike.

New villain

The third movie was called *Austin Powers in Goldmember*. In it Dr. Evil returns with another scheme to take over the world. He plans

to travel back in time and kidnap Austin's father, Nigel Powers. Nigel is played by Michael Caine. Austin must travel back in time again to stop Dr. Evil and a new **villain** called Goldmember. Again, Mike plays Dr. Evil. He also plays Goldmember.

Dr. Evil and Mini Me. Mini Me was played by actor Verne Troyer.

Mike with Heather Graham.

The A-list

Lots of great stars have appeared in the Austin Powers movies. Among the famous names are: Gwyneth Paltrow, Tom Cruise, John Travolta, and Britney Spears. Popular singer Beyoncé Knowles played Austin's sidekick, Foxxy Cleopatra, in *Goldmember*.

Room to grow

The clever thing about these movies is that the characters develop and change. New characters are introduced, such as Mini Me. Old characters are given new life. They are shown earlier in time with younger actors playing them. These changes helped to make the movies a success. The new Austin Powers movies still seemed fresh. The range and number of jokes was much greater. There was no danger of these movies failing in the way that *Wayne's World 2* had done.

Beyoncé Knowles and Michael Caine at the U.S. premiere of *Austin Powers in Goldmember*.

29

Cool cars

It is not just what Austin Powers looked like that helped explain his character. His cars were just as important. What else would Austin Powers drive around in but a Jaguar painted with a Union Jack? When Austin travels back in time in *Austin Powers: The Spy Who Shagged Me*, what kind of car does he make the journey in? The Volkswagen Beetle—a classic symbol of the 1960s and the 1990s.

Mike style

Mike has brought a whole range of different characters to life. Andrew Adamson is a **director** who has worked with Mike. He says: "The thing with Mike is that he's somebody who can really create a character." An important part of creating a character is the clothes they wear. Mike loves dressing up.

Distinctive

Each of Mike's characters has had a very distinctive look. Sometimes the clothes are quite realistic. At other times the clothes are really bizarre.

Realistic

Wayne Campbell is a heavy metal-loving teenager. His ripped jeans and t-shirt are like a uniform. The clothes Mike wore when playing Steve Rubell in *54* are typical of the 1970s, when the movie was set.

Beyoncé Knowles poses next to Austin's car.

Star Words

director person in charge of making a movie
prosthetics false attachments, such as a nose or ears

Some of the outrageous costumes from *Austin Powers in Goldmember*.

★ ★ ★ ★ ★ ★ ★ ★ ★ ★

Cartoon capers

In real life, no one really wore clothes exactly like Austin Powers. What he wears is an over-the-top idea of 1960s' fashion. This adds to the **cartoonish** fun of the character. Fans of the movies love these fun clothes. Some of them even dress up like characters in the movies!

★ ★ ★ ★ ★ ★ ★ ★ ★ ★

Outrageous

In contrast, the clothes of Austin Powers are out of this world. He wears big velvet suits, frilly shirts, and Cuban-heeled boots. Who could forget Austin's Union Jack underwear? All of these clothes match Austin's over-the-top personality.

When you are as popular as Mike, fans come by the busload to see you.

Stick-on bits

Of course, it is not just clothes that make up a character's appearance. Just look at the range of hairstyles Mike has worn on **set**. Mike also uses false teeth and **prosthetics**, like the false nose he wore as Steve Rubell in *54*.

cartoonish like something out of a cartoon

Behind the Scenes

★ ★ ★ ★ ★ ★ ★ ★ ★

Out of the limelight

Mike is very shy. He tries to keep his life as private as possible. An example of this is his pet dogs. Mike has three dogs, but no one seems sure what they are called. One story says they are named after ice hockey players. Another story says he keeps the names secret, so the dogs do not get kidnapped.

★ ★ ★ ★ ★ ★ ★

During the time Mike was working in Chicago, in 1987, he enjoyed going to watch ice hockey. One match he went to was between the Chicago Blackhawks and his local team from Canada, the Toronto Maple Leafs.

Lucky meeting

During the game Mike caught the **puck** when it was accidentally hit into the crowd. Anyone who catches a puck can keep it, so Mike had a fantastic **memento** from the game. Watching the same game was an actress and **scriptwriter** named Robin Ruzan. The story goes that Robin also caught a puck that night—on the head! Mike went to help her. They hit it off and started dating. The couple got married in 1993.

Toronto Maple Leafs are Mike's favorite team.

Star Words

puck small, thick rubber disc used in ice hockey
memento object kept as a reminder or souvenir

Helping hand

Robin has played her part in the success of the Austin Powers movies. She helped Mike write some parts of the movies, most notably the "Just the Two of Us" scene in *Austin Powers: The Spy Who Shagged Me*. Dr. Evil and Mini Me do their own version of this song.

Family joke to TV hit

Robin was not the only member of the Ruzan family to help Mike. He based his popular *Saturday Night Live* character, Linda Richman, on Robin's mother, Linda. Mike used to **impersonate** Linda as a joke for friends and family. Eventually, he tried the character out on *Saturday Night Live*. She was a great success.

Robin, Mike, and Robin's mother, Linda. Linda **inspired** one of Mike's comic characters.

Mike with his wife Robin.

Talk show queen

Linda Richman is the host of a chat show called *Coffee Talk*. Like most of Mike's characters, she has her own **catchphrases**. Linda's most famous one was "I'm verklempt." This is a **Yiddish** expression. It means "I am overcome" or "upset."

Great Gretzky

While Mike was playing Wayne on *Saturday Night Live* in 1989, he had the chance to play hockey against Wayne Gretzky. Gretzky was so good at hockey that he was known as "The Great One." He retired in 1999.

★ ★ ★ ★ ★ ★ ★ ★ ★ ★

Here is ice hockey legend, Wayne Gretzky.

Mike works so hard he does not get a lot of free time. When he gets spare time he uses it on his two great passions: ice hockey and rock music.

Favorite team

The Toronto Maple Leafs is Mike's favorite hockey team. He watches them whenever he can. The Toronto Maple Leafs formed in the 1920s. Their **glory days** were in the 1940s and 1960s when they won the Stanley Cup many times. This is the prize awarded to the champions of the National Hockey League. The last time they won the cup was in 1967. Mike has had a long wait to see further Stanley Cup success.

Ice hockey is the fastest team game in the world. It takes real skill to skate quickly.

Dedicated

Mike likes playing ice hockey, too. When he was taking a break from movies before writing the first Austin Powers movie, he tried to improve his game. He learned how to be a better skater so he could be a better player. That takes **dedication**.

Tea time

Mike also loves music and even plays in a band. The group is called Ming Tea and also includes Susanna Hoffs. She was the lead singer and guitarist with the famous girl group, The Bangles.

Star Words   glory days successful times

Ming Tea has released two singles. They were called "BBC" and "Daddy Wasn't There." Both songs featured in Austin Powers movies. Ming Tea played some of the music in the Austin Powers movies. They also feature in small breaks in the filming. The band was invited to be the house band at Johnny Depp's nightclub, The Viper Room, in Los Angeles.

Folk lover

Mike does not just love rock music. One of his favorite performers is folk singer, Joni Mitchell. She is also a fellow Canadian.

Jay Roach on set with Mike as Austin Powers.

Austin Powers with Ming Tea.

Friends in high places

Jay Roach is a friend of Mike's and a big hockey fan, too. He was the **director** of the Austin Powers films. After making *Austin Powers: International Man of Mystery,* he went on to make a movie about ice hockey called *Mystery, Alaska.* Guess who had a small role in the movie? Ice hockey fan and friend Mike Myers!

dedication working hard at something

Difficult to work with?

No one doubts that Mike is a very hard-working professional. Not everyone agrees that Mike is an easy person to work with, though. When Mike was at Second City, he was not an ideal coworker. Other comedians there remember that he did not want to be part of a team. No one could deny that Mike was very good at what he did, however.

Sprockets

No matter what people thought of Mike, no one expected him to end up with legal problems. This is what happened when Mike agreed to make a movie about another one of his *Saturday Night Live* characters. It was about the character Dieter. Mike was going to write and star in it. The movie was going to be called *Sprockets*.

About turn

Mike soon hit a problem. No matter how many times he rewrote the script, he never thought it was funny enough. He took a hard decision. He pulled out of the movie. The studio that was making the film was Universal. They were not happy with Mike's decision and decided to **sue** him. Mike then decided to sue Universal. He claimed that they had treated him badly. Neither Mike nor Universal would back down. Someone was needed to sort out the mess. That man was Jeffrey Katzenberg.

Star Words   sue go to court to get money from someone

A deal

Katzenberg was one of the owners of another studio called DreamWorks SKG. The studio had links with Mike and with Universal. A deal was reached. Universal would stop suing Mike if he made a different movie for them. Both sides were happy with the deal. Universal would get a Mike Myers movie. Mike would be free from legal battles to make new movies.

Leonardo di Caprio starred in the DreamWorks movie *Catch Me if You Can*.

Dream workers

DreamWorks SKG was set up by Steven Spielberg, Jeffrey Katzenberg, and David Geffen in 1994. The studio has produced many hit movies, such as *Catch Me if You Can* and *Antz*.

Here is Mike with DreamWorks chief, Jeffrey Katzenberg.

A Monster Hit

Cameron Diaz,
the voice of Fiona.

★ ★ ★ ★ ★ ★ ★ ★ ★

The plot

Shrek is an ogre who wants to be left alone. The evil ruler, Lord Farquaad, has overrun Shrek's swamp with fairytale characters. Shrek agrees to rescue Fiona, the woman Farquaad wants to marry, from a dragon. In return, Farquaad agrees to remove the fairytale **"squatters."** But, Fiona loves Shrek, not Farquaad, and she has a secret: she is really an ogre.

★ ★ ★ ★ ★ ★ ★ ★ ★

The end of the legal dispute meant Mike could **promote** the movie he had made for the DreamWorks studio. The movie was called *Shrek*. The surprising thing was that Mike would not be seen on the movie. It was an **animated movie**. Mike had been hired for his voice.

Monster man

Mike provided the voice for the movie's main character, an ogre called Shrek. Mike was not the only star to work on the movie. Other voices were provided by Cameron Diaz, Eddie Murphy, and John Lithgow. Mike also provided the voice for one of the three blind mice in the movie.

All change

When the movie was finished everyone was very happy with the result. Well, nearly everyone.

The main characters from *Shrek*:
Donkey, Shrek, Fiona, and Farquaad.

Star Words

animated movie movie made using drawings, puppets, or computer graphics instead of actors

Mike was not happy. He did not feel that his voice for Shrek was funny enough. Mike was convinced that it would be funnier if the character had a Scottish accent. The **directors** of the movie agreed.

Expensive

To change the recording at this stage would be very expensive. Surprisingly, Jeffrey Katzenberg said it would be all right. Two weeks later the **voiceover** was recorded again and the movie was ready. Jeffrey Katzenberg was right to let Mike rerecord his lines. He knew the movie was good, and was sure it would be a success. It was. You could say the movie was a monster hit!

Perfect combination

DreamWorks studios had animation hits before with movies like *Antz*. It worked well because it mixed fantastic animation with top actors' voices. The script was funny and appealed to both adults and children. *Shrek* worked for exactly the same reasons. The animation was **cutting edge** and the jokes had audiences laughing. Mike had starred in another hit movie.

Mike's highest earning movies

Shrek:
£482.7 million

The Spy Who Shagged Me:
£310.9 million

Goldmember:
£296.6 million

Wayne's World:
£183.1 million

Austin Powers:
£67.7 million

Mike with a model of his character, Shrek.

The Cat in the Hat

Who was Dr. Seuss?

Dr. Seuss wrote *The Cat in the Hat*. His real name was Theodor Seuss Geisel. He was born in 1904. He wrote more than 40 books for children. He wrote such classics as *Green Eggs and Ham*, *Too Many Daves*, and *The Cat in the Hat Comes Back*. Dr. Seuss died in 1991.

★ ★ ★ ★ ★ ★ ★ ★

Back in 2000, Jeffrey Katzenberg sorted out a legal problem between Mike and Universal Studios. As part of that deal, Mike agreed to make a new movie for Universal. In 2003 that movie was released.

Hat-wearing hero

The movie sees Mike playing a brand new character. This time the character was not one of Mike's own inventions. This one was a children's book classic. Mike was playing Dr. Seuss' famous Cat in the Hat.

It took a long time in make-up, but Mike looks great as the Cat in the Hat.

Star Words　　anarchic no respect for rules

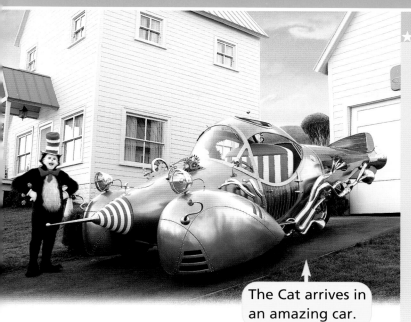

The Cat arrives in an amazing car.

Suffering for his movie

Mike has always used makeup and costumes to help create a character. The costume for *The Cat in the Hat*, was hot, as well as uncomfortable. Even going to the bathroom was difficult.

What a mess

The book *The Cat in the Hat* tells of a magical, **anarchic** cat who wears a big, stripy top hat. When two children sit watching the rain on a cold, wet day, the cat turns up. He tries to entertain the children with games. Instead, he brings **chaos** to the house.

"To play the Cat is a great honor," says Mike.

Madcap Mike

The story is funny and silly with lots of **madcap** humor. It is an ideal role for Mike, who loves the whole idea of being silly. Unlike *Shrek*, *The Cat in the Hat* is not **animated**. Instead it is live action. This means that Mike has to be turned into the character of the cat. To do this Mike had to spend three hours each day in make-up.

★ **Star fact**

The Cat in the Hat is one of the best-selling children's books of all time.

madcap crazy

Future Plans

★ ★ ★ ★ ★ ★ ★ ★ ★ ★

Home lover

Mike is very proud of being a Canadian. Mike says: "Toronto is always home. There's a certain attitude there that doesn't exist anywhere else."

★ ★ ★ ★ ★ ★ ★ ★ ★ ★

Mike happily signs autographs for fans.

Mike has been very successful. Now he can afford to pick and choose what he does next. Perhaps he will invent another new character. He may take more acting roles like the one he played in *54* or the more recent film, *View From the Top*.

Animated return

Busy actors like Mike always have work. In 2004, *Shrek 2* was released. The movie features Mike's **costars** from the first movie, Cameron Diaz and Eddie Murphy. The plot for this movie sees Shrek and Fiona travelling to the kingdom of Far, Far Away to visit Fiona's parents. They have lots of adventures on the way.

Star Words   SARS virus fast-spreading disease that killed people in 2003

Other movies

Mike had a guest role in *View From the Top* in 2003. He has also been in two other movies called *McClintock's Peach* and *Pete's Meteor*. Both movies had good reviews at previews, but neither had found a **distributor** in 2004.

Austin Powers 4?

What many fans would like to know is whether there will be another Austin Powers movie. Mike has been reported as saying that he is not keen, but there have been rumors that there may be another movie.

Public support

Mike had not planned for the outbreak of the **SARS virus** in his beloved Toronto in 2003. Mike took time out of his busy schedule to reassure people that Toronto was still a safe place to visit. He even appeared on *The Tonight Show* to **promote** his city.

Extraordinary man

Mike is certainly a busy superstar, but at heart he is still a boy from the **suburbs** who loves his town and is proud of his country. Looking at what he has achieved, he has certainly done "something extraordinary," to quote his own words.

View From the Top star, Gwyneth Paltrow.

distributor company that supplies movies to theaters

Find Out More

Books

Dupont, Lonnie Hull. *Mike Myers.*
Minneapolis: Sagebrush Education
Resources, 2003

Knelman, Martin. *Mike's World: The Life of
Mike Myers.* New York: Firefly Books,
2003

Lane, Andy. *The World of Austin Powers.*
New York: Universe Publishing, 2002

Spielberg, Steven. *Shrek: Essential Guide.*
New York: Dorling Kindersley, 2004

Filmography

Shrek 2 (2004)
The Cat in the Hat (2003)
View From the Top (2003)
Austin Powers in Goldmember (2002)
Shrek (2001)
Mystery, Alaska (1999)
*Austin Powers: The Spy Who
Shagged Me* (1999)
54 (1998)
*Austin Powers: International Man
of Mystery* (1997)
Wayne's World 2 (1993)
So I Married an Axe Murderer (1993)
Wayne's World (1992)
Range Rider and the Calgary Kid (1977)

Television

Saturday Night Live (1989–1995)
It's Only Rock and Roll (1987)
The Wide Awake Club (1985)

Website search tips

There are billions of pages on the Internet so it can be difficult to find exactly what you are looking for. If you just type in "movie" on a search engine like Google, you will get a list of millions of web pages. These search skills will help you find useful websites more quickly:

- know exactly what you want to find out
- use simple keywords, not whole sentences
- use two to six keywords in a search
- be precise, only use names of people, places or things
- if you want to find words that go together, put quote marks around them
- use the "+" sign to add certain words, for example typing "Mike Myers + movies" into the search box will find web pages about Mike's movies.

Glossary

adapt make changes because of differing circumstances

anarchic no respect for rules

animated movie movie made using drawings, puppets, or computer graphics instead of actors

audition interview for an actor or musician, where they show their skills

broadcast transmit by radio or television

cartoonish like something out of a cartoon

catchphrase saying linked with a certain character

chaotic confused and lacking order

cockney people from East London, in England are called cockneys

commercial success something that sells well and makes a good profit

costars actors appearing together in a film or television show

cutting edge newest way of doing something

daunting when a task seems hard or scary

dedication working hard at something

director person in charge of making a movie

distributor company that supplies movies to theaters

emigrate to leave one country and move to another

Emmy Award important American television award

formative years years that shape your character

glory days successful times

impersonate copy or imitate

improvise make things up as you go along

inconsolable unable to be cheered up

inspiration where you get your ideas from

madcap crazy

memento object kept as a reminder or souvenir

prestigious having a good reputation

producer person who organizes the people and the money to make a movie or television show

promote tell people about a new product

propellant fuel

prosthetics false attachments such as a nose or ears

puck small, thick rubber disc used in ice hockey

rehearsal practice

SARS virus fast-spreading disease that killed people in 2003

screening early preview of a movie

scriptwriter someone who writes scripts for movies, television programs or commercials

sequel follow up

set part of a movie studio where a movie or commercial is shot

slapstick people falling over or being hit in a funny way

squatter someone who takes over your house and lives there when you do not want them to

suburbs outskirts of a town or city where people live

sue go to court to get money from someone

troupe group of performers

variety show mixture of songs, dances, and comedy

veteran person with a lot of experience in something

villain character who is bad

voiceover voice given to a cartoon character

Yiddish Jewish language or dialect

Index

Adamson, Andrew 30
Aerosmith 16
Aykroyd, Dan 10

Bangles, The 35
Barr, Roseanne 17
Barrymore, Drew 8
Beatles, The 7
Belushi, James 15

Caine, Michael 28
Candy, John 10
Caprio, Leonardo di 37
Carvey, Dana 14–15, 24
Chase, Chevy 15
Cruise, Tom 29

Depp, Johnny 35
DeVito, Danny 16
Diaz, Cameron 38, 42
DreamWorks 37–39

Ferrell, Will 15
Foster, Jodie 8

Geffen, David 37
Goodman, John 16
Graham, Heather 28, 29
Gretzky, Wayne 16, 34

Hanks, Tom 16
Hoffs, Susanna 35
Hurley, Elizabeth 27

Jagger, Mick 16

Katzenberg, Jeffrey 36–40
Knowles, Beyoncé 29–30

Levy, Eugene 10
Lithgow, John 38
Lowe, Rob 18

Madonna 17
Michaels, Lorne 14–15
Ming Tea 35
Mitchell, Joni 35
Moore, Demi 26
Mullarkey, Neil 11, 20
Murphy, Eddie 15, 38, 42
Murray, Bill 10
Myers, Eric 4, 22, 23
Myers, Mike
    auditions 8, 10
    awards 15
    books 44
    childhood 6–10
    hobbies 34–35
    marriage 32–33
    movies 25, 30–31, 42
    Austin Powers
        26–28, 35, 39
    The Cat in the Hat
        40–41
    Goldmember 28–29, 39
    McClintock's Peach 43
    Mystery, Alaska 35
    Pete's Meteor 43
    Range Rider and the
        Calgary Kid 9
    Shrek 38–39, 41
    Shrek 2 42–43
    So I Married an
        Axe Murderer 20
    Sprockets 36
    The Spy Who
        Shagged Me 28, 30,
        33, 39
    View From the Top 42
    Wayne's World 4, 12,
        18–22, 24, 39
    Wayne's World 2
        20–21, 28–29
    parents 4, 6–7, 22–23

television
    It's Only Rock and
        Roll 12–13
    Mullarkey and
        Myers 11
    Saturday Night Live 4,
        8–9, 14–19, 21, 24,
        33–34
    The Tonight Show 43
    The Wide Awake
        Club 11

Paltrow, Gwyneth 29, 43

Radner, Gilda 8–9
Ricci, Christina 8
Roach, Jay 35
Ruzan, Linda 33
Ruzan, Robin 32

Sandler, Adam 15
Second City 10–14, 36
Sellers, Peter 22
Seuss, Dr. 40
Spears, Britney 29
Spielberg, Steven 37
Steig, William 39
Streisand, Barbra 17

Travis, Nancy 21
Travolta, John 29

Universal Studios 36, 37, 40

Willis, Bruce 16